SHREDDING BACH

HEAVY METAL GUITAR MEETS 10 J.S. BACH MASTERPIECES

GERMAN SCHAUSS

Alfred, the leader in educational publishing,
and the National Guitar Workshop,
one of America's finest guitar schools, have joined
forces to bring you the best, most progressive
educational tools possible. We hope you will enjoy
this book and encourage you to look for
other fine products from Alfred and the
National Guitar Workshop.

This book was acquired, edited and produced
by Workshop Arts, Inc., the publishing arm of
the National Guitar Workshop.
Nathaniel Gunod, acquisitions, managing editor
Burgess Speed, acquisitions, senior editor
Timothy Phelps, interior design
Ante Gelo, music typesetter
CD recorded by German Schauss

Guitar on cover courtesy Schecter Guitar Research
Baroque ornament: © iStockphoto / Scott Krycia

Alfred Music Publishing Co., Inc.
P.O. Box 10003
Van Nuys, CA 91410-0003
alfred.com

ISBN-10: 0-7390-6951-9 (Book & CD)
ISBN-13: 978-0-7390-6951-6 (Book & CD)

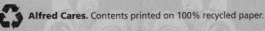

Alfred Cares. Contents printed on 100% recycled paper.

TABLE OF CONTENTS

1

A compact disc is available with this book. Using the disc will help make learning more enjoyable and the information more meaningful. Listening to the CD will help you correctly interpret the rhythms and feel of each example. The symbol to the left appears next to each song or example that is performed on the CD. The track number below each symbol corresponds directly to the example you want to hear. Track 1 will help you tune to this CD.

ABOUT THE AUTHOR

German Schauss is a guitarist, composer, author, and educator who teaches at Berklee College of Music and the Los Angeles Music Academy. He performs and tours as the leader of his own band and with other internationally known artists. Schauss is a clinician for music companies such as Parker Guitars and performs at trade shows around the world. He writes music for commercials, TV, and video games, and has been named one of the 50 fastest guitarists of all time by Guitar World Magazine.

PHOTO BY JI YEON SONG

He also writes his very popular monthly column "Instant Shredding" for Germany's biggest guitar magazine Gitarre & Bass.

German uses and proudly endorses: Parker Guitars, Bogner Amplifiers, DiMarzio, Rocktron, DR Strings, PreSonus, Native Instruments, Maxon, Guyatone, Morley, Dunlop, Voodoo Lab, and Pedaltrain products.

For more about German Schauss and his music, please visit:

www.germanschauss.com

Acknowledgements

First and foremost, I would like to thank my wife, Ji Yeon, for her never-ending patience, guidance, and love. Furthermore, I thank my mother, Renate, my father, Juergen, my brother, Roman, my sister-in-law, Ursula, my grandmother, Inge, and grandfather, Josef, for their love and belief in me and my music. Additionally, I would like to thank Burgess Speed at Workshop Arts, and Link Harnsberger and Aaron Stang at Alfred Music Publishing, for their help and support. I would also like to thank all my friends and fans around the world for their support, positive thoughts, and love.

INTRODUCTION

J. S. Bach (1685–1750) is considered one of the greatest composers and musicians of all time. This makes his amazing compositions a perfect match for heavy metal, or shred, guitar.

Included in this book are 10 very interesting and challenging J. S. Bach pieces adapted for shred guitar. You will find that each piece presents different challenges. You will not only learn about the music of this great master but will also learn to incorporate different modern guitar techniques into your playing, such as sweep picking, tapping, legato, and rapid alternate picking.

The arrangements here are as true to the original compositions as possible. Only certain measures and endings have been modified to fit into the style of shred guitar.

For your reference and practice, this book contains a CD featuring all the lead guitar arrangements—with accompanying rhythm section—at a normal, fast pace. Additionally, there are two backing tracks (minus the lead guitar) for each piece—one at a much slower pace and one at the normal, fast tempo.

Shredding Bach is for intermediate to advanced guitarists who can read standard music notation or TAB and have a firm grasp on basic guitar technique and music theory (scale theory, diatonic harmony, etc.). However, you do not already have to be a "shred" guitarist to benefit from this book. As you learn each new piece, you will also be introduced to the shred techniques required to play it.

The music of J. S. Bach is universal. It can be adapted to many different instruments, but the virtuosity and power required for shred guitar makes it a natural fit. I hope you enjoy these fresh interpretations and that they help you to grow as a musician.

Johann Sebastian Bach (1685–1750).

INVENTION NO. 8 IN F MAJOR

Brief Musical Analysis

Bach's "Invention No. 8 in F Major" (BWV 779)* is probably one of the most well-known compositions in music history. The melody is easily recognizable because of its *triadic* opening. ("Triadic" just refers to "triads," or three-note chords.) This invention starts out in the key of F Major and slowly *modulates* (changes keys) to C Major in measure 12. C is the *dominant* key, or the key of the 5th scale degree of the *tonic* key (which is the key of the 1st scale degree). In other words, there are seven scale degrees in a major scale: 1–2–3–4–5–6–7. Each scale degree refers to a note of the scale, for instance: F(1)–G(2)–A(3)–B♭(4)–C(5)–D(6)–E(7). As you can see, the tonic, or key of the 1st scale degree, would be F Major, and the dominant, or key of the 5th scale degree, would be C Major. The triadic theme is repeated again in measure 13, this time in the new key of C.

After that, the piece modulates through different chords to the *relative minor* (the chord built on the 6th scale degree of the tonic key, in this case, D Minor) and continues to modulate back to the dominant chord (C) of the original key (F). Measures 29 through 32 lead the listener back to the final *cadence* (ending) in measure 33, which concludes with an F Major chord in *1st inversion* (meaning the 3rd is in the bass). The piece also features several different technical challenges such as arpeggios, scale sequences, alternate picking, and pedal tones. This next section will discuss some of these techniques.

Arpeggios

The example below shows an F Major arpeggio. An arpeggio is a "broken chord," or the notes of a chord played individually rather than simultaneously. The piece features several arpeggiated sections in F Major, C Major, G Major, G Minor, D Minor, and B♭ Major.

Measure 1

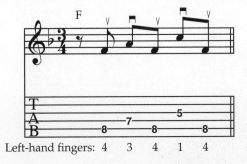

Left-hand fingers: 4 3 4 1 4

* BWV is the abbreviation for *Bach-Werke-Verzeichnis,* or "Bach Works Catalog."
Each piece in Bach's catalog of works is identified by number.

The example below shows a variation of the arpeggiated triad starting on beat 1.

Measure 16

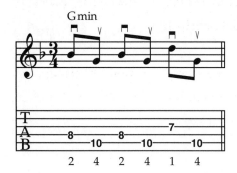

There are several other triadic variations throughout the piece, like in measures 1, 3, 7, 11, 13, 16, and 18. Practice all of these variations before working on the piece as a whole. These arpeggiated sections are an important part of the piece, and if you have already mastered them, they will fall nicely into place when you tackle the piece in its entirety. Don't forget to play these different triadic figures in the keys mentioned on the previous page.

Scale Sequences

The example below is a short scale *sequence* (pattern, or phrase, repeated at different pitch levels) with a repetitive fingering pattern (4–3–1–3, 4–3–1–3, etc.) Similar sequences occur in measures 8–10, 14, 17, and 30–32.

Measure 2

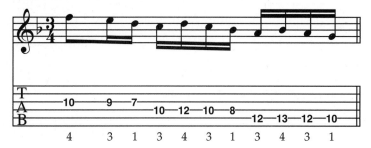

Alternate Picking

Alternate picking is the technique of alternating your picking direction (⊓∨⊓∨ etc.) with each new note. The example below shows a basic phrase (not an excerpt from the invention). Practice this pattern over and over for great alternate-picking control and synchronization between your right and left hands.

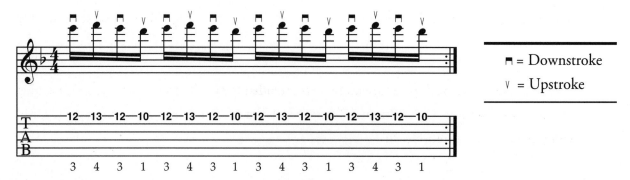

⊓ = Downstroke

∨ = Upstroke

Pedal Tones

A *pedal tone* is a note that is repeated against notes of ascending or descending scales, or arpeggiation. (In the example below, the pedal tone is highlighted.)

Practice the following example (which is based on measure 4 of the invention) using strict alternate picking. Try moving it up on the string while maintaining the key of F Major. Also, try moving the pattern to different strings and even different keys.

Measure 4

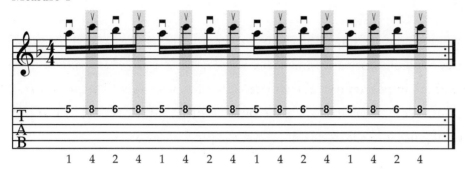

The example below shows a variation of a pedal-tone phrase that can be found in measure 15. In this phrase, the repeating note is preceded by a short, three-note phrase that includes the 3rd of the chord that is being outlined.

Measure 15

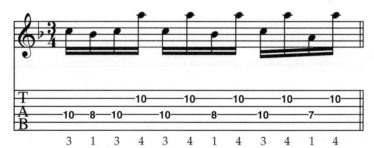

A similar pedal-tone phrase occurs in measures 21, 22, and 23. The harmonies depicted in these measures are C7, F, and A7, respectively. Practice these phrases very carefully, as they can be quite challenging to play accurately and cleanly.

Final Words of Preparation

Bach's "Invention No. 8 in F Major" is a fun piece and a great chops builder. Practice it slowly and try to memorize the different skips and position changes, as this will help you to eventually perform the piece at faster tempos.

Listen to Track 2 to hear the entire piece at its intended tempo. Tracks 3 and 4 are the backing tracks (minus guitar). Track 3 is at full speed and Track 4 is at a much slower tempo. Now, enjoy Bach's "Invention No. 8!"

INVENTION NO. 8 IN F MAJOR

Backing Tracks
3—Fast
4—Slow

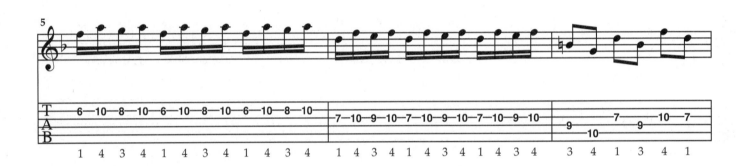

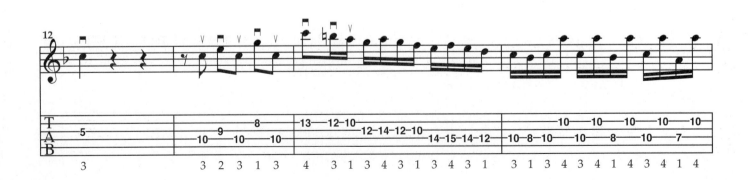

SHREDDING BACH

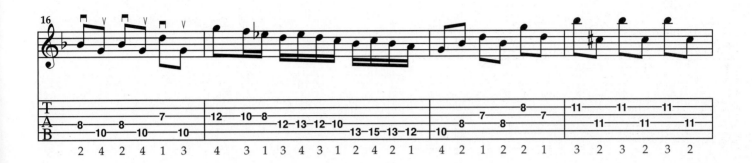

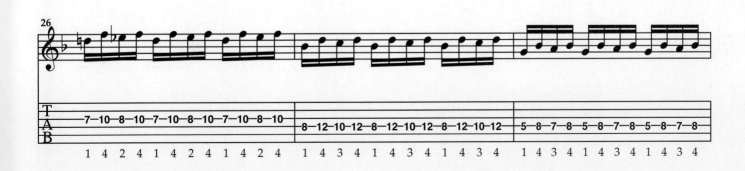

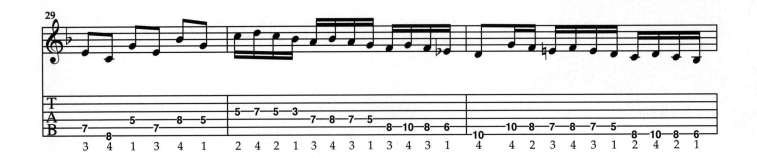

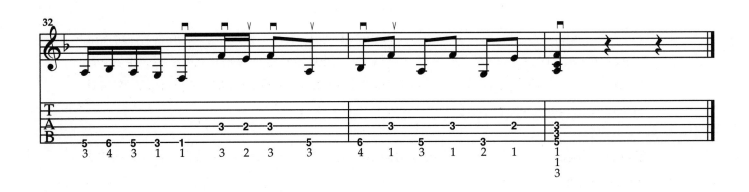

DOUBLE IN B MINOR

Brief Musical Analysis

Bach's "Double in B Minor" (BWV 1002) is originally from his collection of *Sonatas and Partitas for Solo Violin.* This piece is a great challenge to perform on guitar, as it requires a lot of string skipping (see page 12) and other complex movements.

The harmonic outline of the first half of this piece is relatively simple. It starts in B Minor and moves through the diatonic chords in that key until measure 6, where it targets the iv chord (E Minor) with a dominant chord (B7). It modulates to the dominant key in measure 11, and then ends on the V chord (F♯7) of the tonic key in measure 12.

The piece begins with a pickup note and leads into a B Minor arpeggio, followed by an F♯7 dominant phrase.

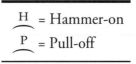

H = Hammer-on
P = Pull-off

Measure 1

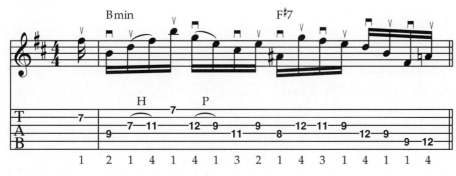

Sweep Picking

Most of this piece is played using alternate picking, but there are occasional passages played with hammer-ons, pull-offs, and *sweep picking*. Sweep picking is a technique where the pick is "swept" across adjacent strings in a downward or upward motion while the left hand frets each note individually and releases it as the next note is played. This creates a fluid-sounding series of individual notes rather than a chord.

The following measure is a good example of the sweep picking that will occur in this piece. The "sweeping" begins on the second sixteenth note of beat 3 and ends on the first sixteenth note of beat 4. The rest of the phrase is played using alternate picking. Practice the following example, paying close attention to the picking directions.

Measure 3

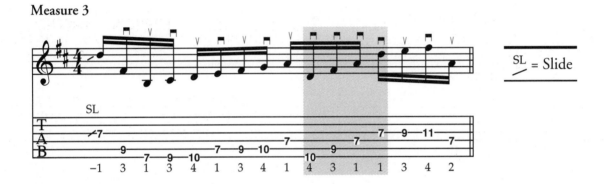

String Skipping

This piece also requires a lot of *string skipping* in order to accommodate the different melodic lines. The term "string skipping" just refers to the technique of playing passages that require you to jump over, or skip, strings.

The next example illustrates the use of string skipping, hammer-ons, and pull-offs. Be sure to use the fingering indicated under the TAB, as this will help you play the challenging passages more easily.

Measure 7

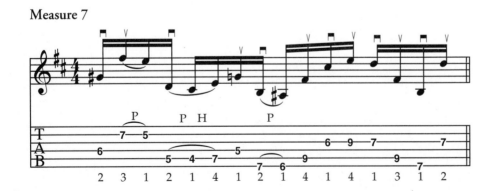

String Skipping and Sweep Picking Combined

Some passages combine string sweeping and sweep picking. The final two measures of this piece are a great example of this. These two measures are probably the most challenging in this piece, as they require large melodic skips and perfect left- and right-hand synchronization. The implied harmony for measure 11 is a C#7♭9 chord that leads into the F#7 chord in measure 12. C#7♭9 is the *secondary dominant* of F#7. A secondary dominant is a dominant chord built on the 5th degree above any chord other than the tonic (C# is a 5th above F#, which is the dominant chord in the tonic key, B Minor), and it creates a greater "pull" toward the chord it is resolving to. Watch the slide on the first note of measure 11.

Measures 11–12

It is very common in music to modulate, or change from the starting key, to either the key of the dominant (remember, this is the key of the 5th scale degree) or the relative major or minor. This provides the composer with more tonal possibilities and interesting compositional ideas.

Once you have mastered the first part of this piece and are interested in learning more on your own, try arranging the second part using the techniques covered in this section. (It is very easy to find the original music online or in books.) This is a great learning experience and will enhance your guitar technique immensely.

You can hear this arrangement played with a full band on Track 5. Tracks 6 and 7 are backing tracks minus guitar.

DOUBLE IN B MINOR

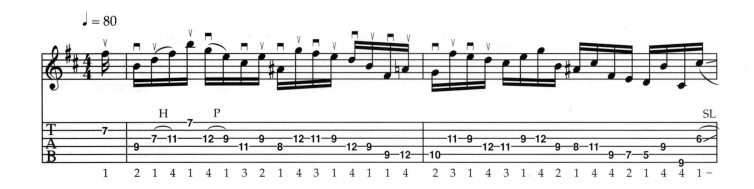

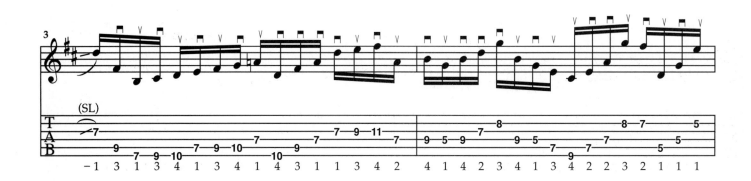

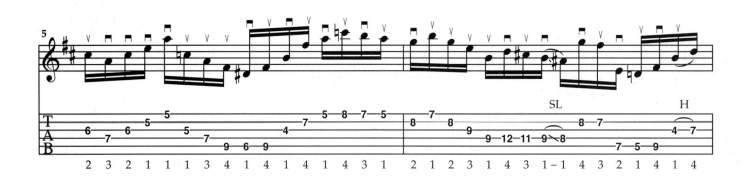

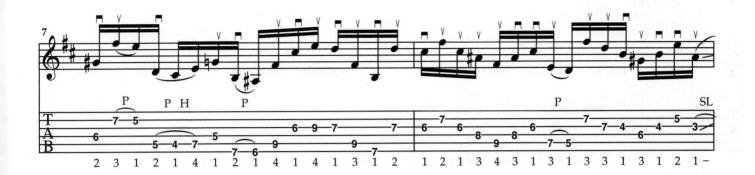

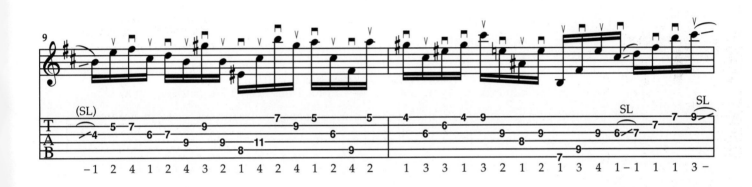

PRESTO IN G MINOR

Brief Musical Analysis

The "Presto in G Minor" (BWV 1001) is from the collection of *Sonatas and Partitas for Solo Violin.* It is a fast piece in $\frac{3}{8}$ time (which means there are three beats per measure with the eighth note receiving the beat). This composition was arranged in a way that encompasses a lot of different guitar techniques, such as sweeping, tapping (see page 17), alternate picking, and string skipping. It is a real challenge, but well worth the results. Let's start by breaking down the more difficult passages.

Arpeggios

The example below is an excerpt from measures 1–4 and is a simple G Minor arpeggio played in a descending three-note sequence. This is a very common arpeggio treatment found in Baroque and Classical music. Practice it slowly and accurately, and strive for a clean sound.

Measures 1–4

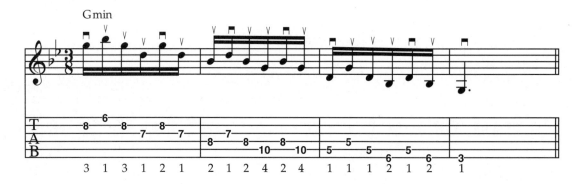

Now, practice the passage above in different positions, and try changing the chord type to major, diminished, augmented, etc.

Ascending 4ths

The example below consists of measures 12 and 13 of "Presto in G Minor." It is an excerpt from a longer ascending sequence of 4ths. (Note: It is the root notes of the chords being outlined that are ascending in 4ths.) The first measure outlines a D7 chord, which resolves to Gmin7 in the next measure. This sequence continues to ascend in 4ths to C Minor, F Major, B♭ Major, and finally, E♭ Major in measures 17–18. Pay close attention to the picking directions, as well as the areas with string skipping, as this is vital to a smooth performance of this passage.

Measures 12–13

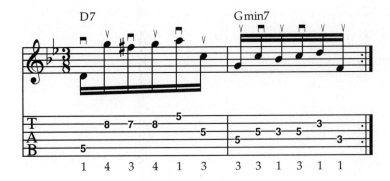

Tapping

The following excerpt (measures 17 and 18) is based on a *2nd inversion* (5th in the bass) E♭ Major arpeggio, played using the *tapping* technique. Tapping was first introduced by Edward Van Halen in the late 1970s. It utilizes the fingers of the picking hand to "tap" a note (or notes) against the fretboard at the appropriate fret. Often, the tapping finger then pulls off to a note already fingered by the left hand.

To play the example below, tap the first note on the 6th string with your right-hand middle finger (m) and pull it off to the 3rd finger of your left hand. Tap again, then hammer your left-hand 1st finger onto the 5th fret of the 4th string. Tap again on the 6th string, and hammer again with the left hand onto the 5th fret of the 4th string. Continue this pattern for the next measure. Practice this idea across the entire fretboard, trying it on different sets of strings. The arpeggio is moved to F Major in measures 19–20 and changes to a slightly different tapping pattern for the E♭ and F Major arpeggios in measures 21–24.

Measures 17–18

T = Tap

m = right-hand middle finger

The example below is a short excerpt from a pedal-tone sequence (measures 25–28), this time arranged for tapping.

Do not use your pick at all in this example. Using the *hammer-on-from-nowhere* technique, sound the first note by pressing against the string with your left-hand 1st finger. Then hammer onto the second note and tap the third one with your right hand. After that, use your fretting hand to play the pedal phrase on the 2nd string. All of this is accomplished by hammering-on, pulling-off, and tapping. Remember, no pick is used. This requires skill and will take some practice if you are not familiar with this technique.

Measures 25–26

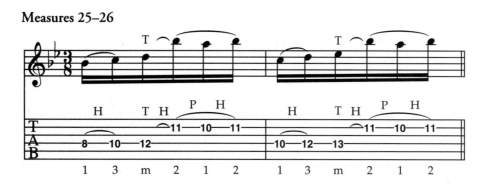

More Excerpts

The excerpt below is part of a more complex sequence starting in measure 35 and ending in measure 42. This two-measure excerpt is the beginning of the eight-bar phrase, which continues in the same way, outlining the chords A7, Dmin, B♭, C7, F, B♭, Emin7♭5, and A7.

Practice the example below using alternate picking, and make sure you play the different chord transitions smoothly.

Measures 35–36

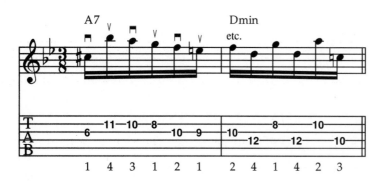

The example below shows a more scale-based approach found in measures 46–51. This should be played with strict alternate picking. Also, make sure you "roll" your left-hand finger when fretting consecutive notes on the same fret but adjacent strings (for example: A to D in the first measure).

Measures 47–48

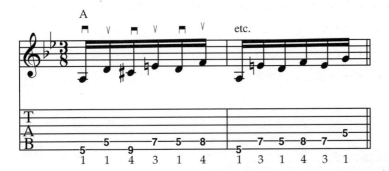

The final measures are arranged to create a more guitar-oriented ending for this piece. It consists of a series of tapped arpeggios progressing from D Minor to A7 and ending with a D Major descending arpeggio. Practice the ending separately before working on the piece in its entirety.

Measures 52–56

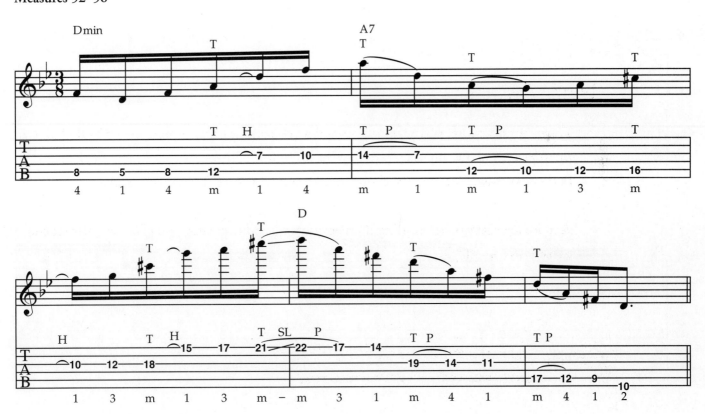

On Track 8 you will find the entire piece. Tracks 9 and 10 are fast and slow backing tracks. Good luck!

Note: At the beginning of the piece on the next page, you will see two tempo indications. The one in parentheses represents the feel recorded on the CD, while the other represents a more traditional tempo marking. Both speeds are identical but can be interpreted differently.

PRESTO IN G MINOR

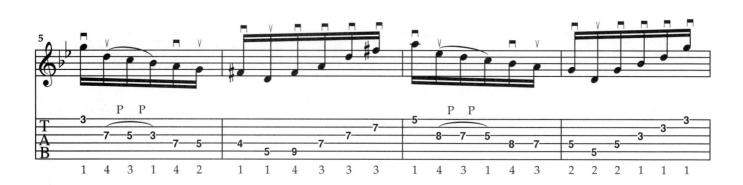

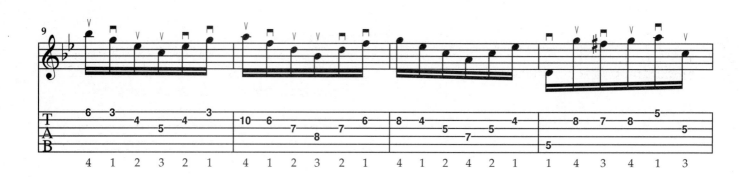

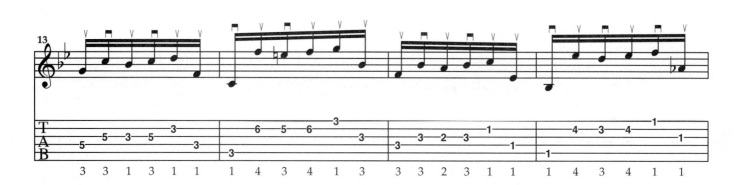

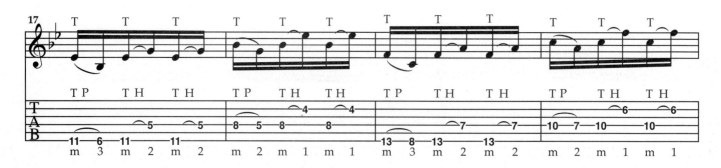

* For an explanation of the two tempo markings, see bottom of page 19.

SHREDDING BACH

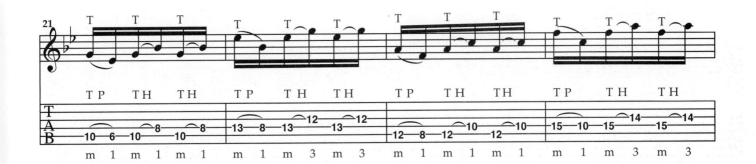

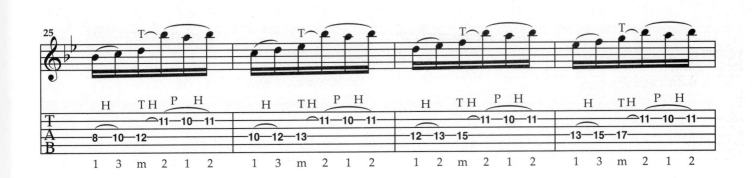

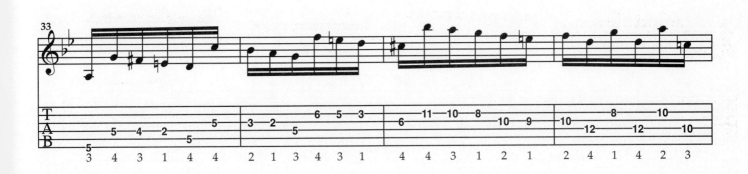

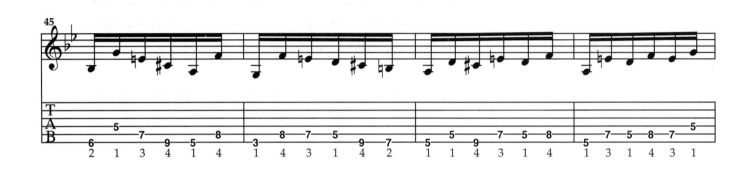

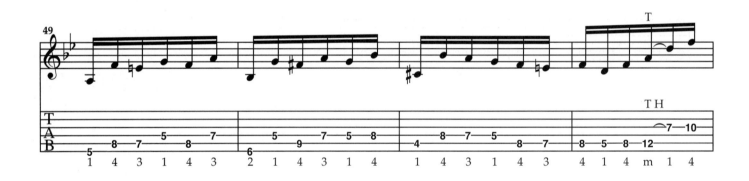

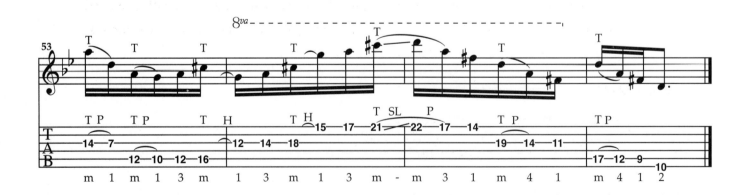

INVENTION NO. 4 IN D MINOR

Brief Musical Analysis

J.S. Bach's "Invention No. 4 in D Minor" (BWV 775) is another well-known piece. The meter is $\frac{3}{8}$, and it is usually performed at a brisk and flowing pace. However, according to some researchers, this piece should be played at a slower, more expressive tempo.

The theme is stated in measures 1 and 2. This theme is repeated in different transpositions throughout the piece (measures 5–6, 26–27, and 44–45).

Measures 1–2

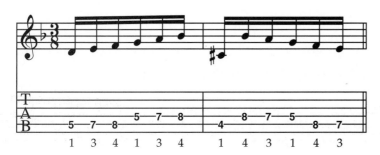

The theme from above is also *inverted* and imitated throughout the piece, either as a complete two-measure phrase or just a one-measure sequence. ("Inverting," in this sense, just means going in opposite directions. Whereas the original theme starts low and ascends, the inverted theme starts high and descends, etc.) The following example is from measures 22–23, and it is an inversion of the theme stated in measures 1 and 2 above.

Measures 22–23

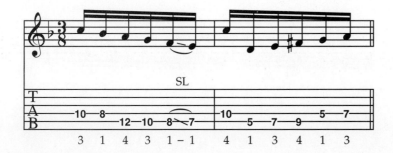

After the theme is repeated one octave higher in measures 5–6, the piece continues with a sequence outlining the chords of D Minor, G Minor, C Major, F Major, D Minor, G Major, C Major, and finally, F Major (measures 7–14). Below is an excerpt from that sequence of chords.

Measures 7–10

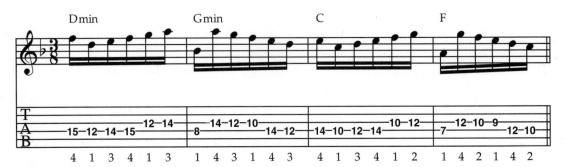

Trills

In measures 19–22, a simple *trill* is played against an underlying harmony of C7, F Major, and G Minor. A trill is a rapid series of hammer-ons and pull-offs between two notes.

In the example below, you are trilling between the notes C and D. First, you will see it as it is written. Then, you will see it as it is to be played.

Measures 19–22

Written:

Played:

You can also trill using a combination of right-hand taps, pull-offs, and hammer-ons. This can help you achieve much faster speeds (and is a great performance move!). The following example demonstrates this alternate approach to trilling that you can try in measures 19-22.

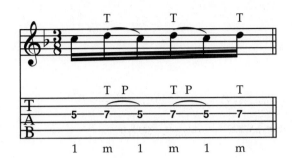

The piece modulates to A Minor in measure 26, after which it continues to run through a series of scale sequences (measures 26–43) similar to what we saw in the beginning. It then modulates back to D Minor and restates the original theme, one octave higher, in measures 44–45.

Measures 44–45

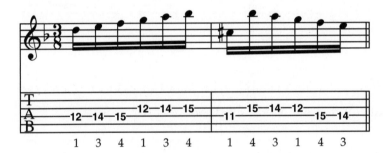

Cadential 6/4

Bach prepares the ending of the piece by alternating between D Minor (i) and the chords A7 (V7) and C♯ Diminished 7 (vii°7). This culminates in a *cadential 6/4* going to A7 and ending on D Minor. A cadential 6/4 is a chord phrase, based on two chords, that is used most commonly at the end of a piece. The first chord is the I chord in 2nd inversion, which is also known as a *I 6/4* chord. (The "6/4" refers to the intervals in the chord as related to the bass note. This system of notation is called *figured bass*. In figured bass, a 6/4 chord is comprised of the intervals of a 6th and a 4th in relation to the bass note. For instance, a I 6/4 chord in the key of D Minor would be spelled A–D–F; from A to F is a 6th, and from A to D is a 4th.) The second chord in a cadential 6/4 is the V chord in root position. (In the key of D Minor, this would be an A chord, spelled A–C♯–E.) This phrase creates a smooth transition to the final chord.

Again, Track 11 is the complete arrangement, and Tracks 12 and 13 are backing tracks for you to practice with.

Note: At the beginning of the piece on the next page, you will see two tempo indications. The one in parentheses represents the feel on the CD, while the other represents a more traditional tempo marking.

INVENTION No. 4 in D Minor

11

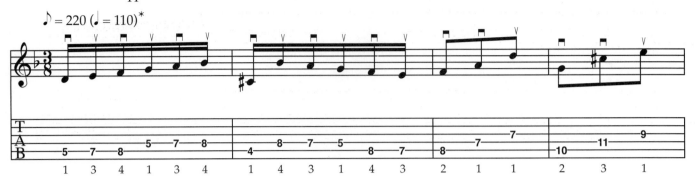

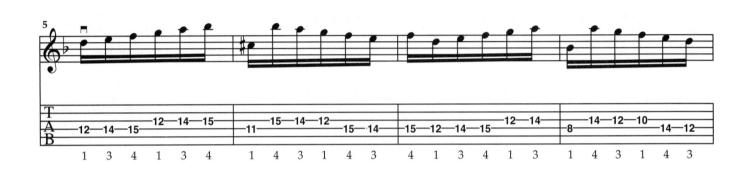

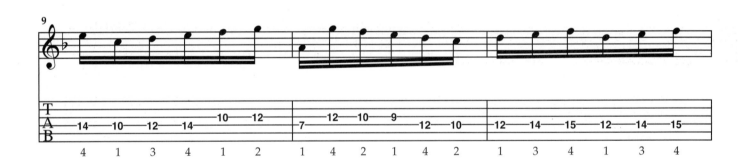

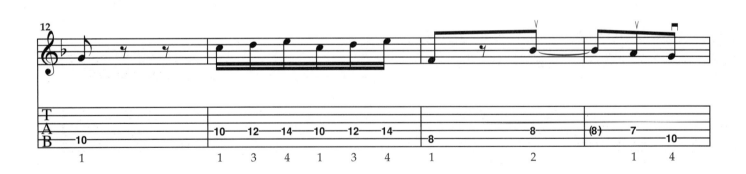

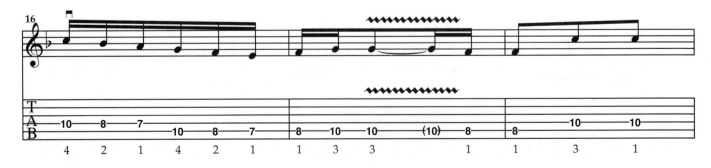

* For an explanation of the two tempo markings, see bottom of page 25.

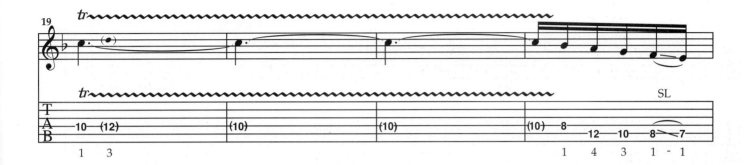

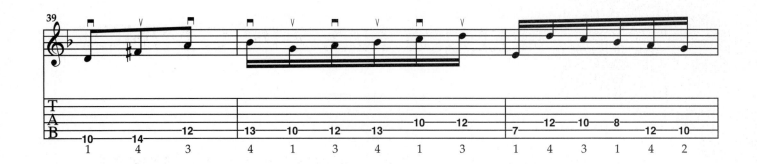

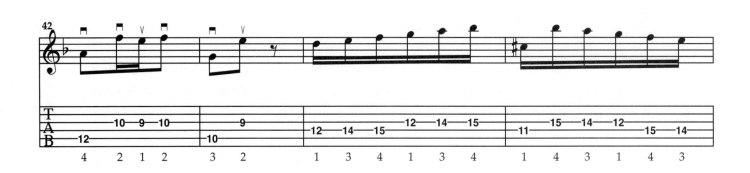

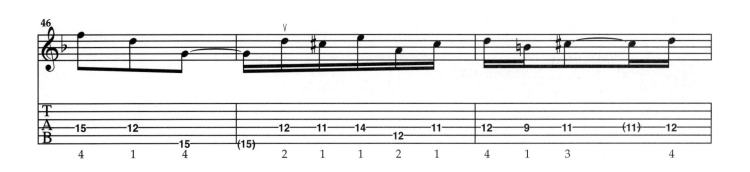

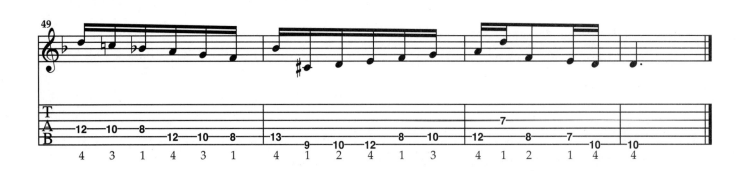

PRELUDE NO. 2 IN C MINOR

Bach's "Prelude No. 2 in C Minor" (BWV 847) is a fast-paced piece that will challenge your alternate picking technique. A *prelude* can be seen as a warm-up exercise before a main piece.

Section 1: Pedal-Tone Phrases

This prelude can be broken down into four sections, the first of which consists of measures 1–24. This first section contains the main motif of this piece, a pedal tone. This piece features basic pedal-tone phrases that either utilize two strings or are spread across three strings.

The example below shows a pedal-tone phrase on two strings. It is played with strict alternate picking. The phrase outlines a C Minor chord and starts with the root.

Measure 1

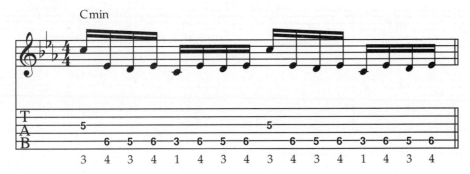

The following example illustrates a similar pedal-tone phrase but with the notes distributed over three strings. This pedal tone outlines an F Minor chord, starting with the minor 3rd of the chord.

Measure 2

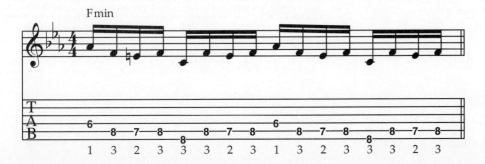

The harmonic development of the first 24 bars is relatively simple, as the general prelude form does not have a set harmonic scheme or progression. It moves freely from C Minor to its relative major key (E$^\flat$) and back to C Minor.

Section 2: Arpeggios

The next section—measures 25 through 27—is a big exception to this mostly scale-based piece, as it consists of a series of arpeggios. The chord progression in this section is G7♭9 to C Minor to F♯ Diminished.

This section employs a mixture of alternate picking and sweep picking. This is probably the most difficult section of the entire piece, as it is not based on a repetitive phrase. Remember, sweeping is a picking technique that utilizes the direction of your picking hand with combined downstrokes or upstrokes. In this piece, the notes in the sweeping sections have been arranged in one-note-per-string patterns to facilitate easier sweeping.

Practice this section separately and slowly to ensure the correct use of these techniques before playing it faster; accuracy enables you to develop speed.

Measures 25–27

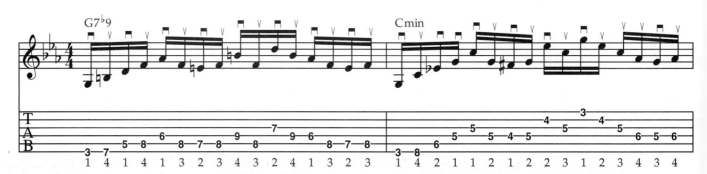

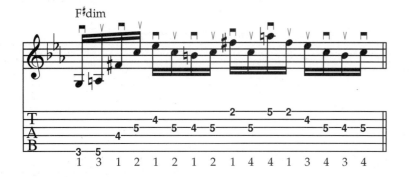

Section 3: Position Shifting and More Pedal-Tone Phrases

The third section (measures 28–34) is again based on a pedal-tone idea, but it is more complex than section 1. There is more scalar and harmonic movement within the phrases, as well as more position shifting on the fretboard.

Pay close attention to the correct fingering in the exercise below, as it will help you shift effortlessly between the different positions without sacrificing speed and accuracy.

Measures 28–29

Section 4: Cadence and the Picardy 3rd

The last four measures constitute the *cadence,* or ending, of the piece and are also played with a mixture of alternate picking and sweeping.

The piece ends with the major 3rd (E) of the C Major chord. When you change the quality of the 3rd from minor to major at the end of a section or piece, it is known as the *Picardy 3rd.* This is a very common stylistic element of the Baroque period.

Measures 35–38

Try to isolate the challenging parts and practice them slowly before attempting the entire piece. This prelude is a great exercise for developing left- and right-hand coordination and technique.

On Track 14, you will find the entire arrangement. Tracks 15 and 16 are fast and slow backing tracks for you to practice over.

Prelude No. 2 in C Minor

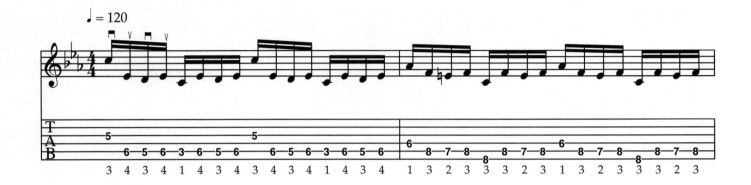

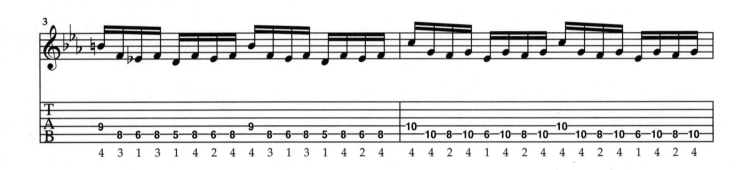

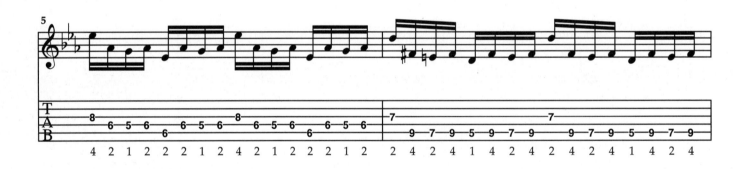

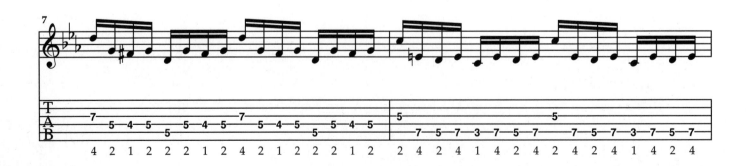

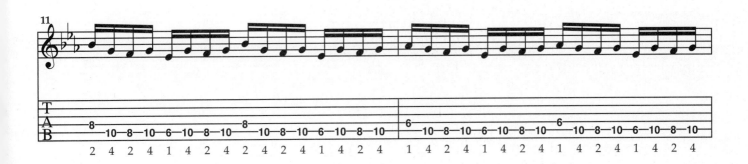

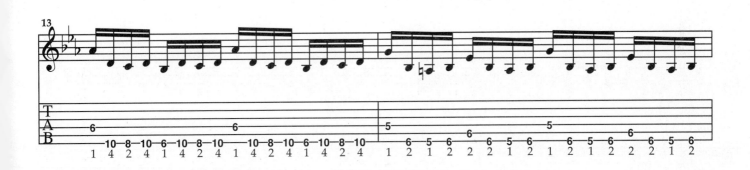

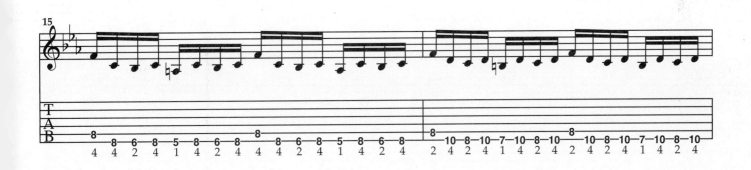

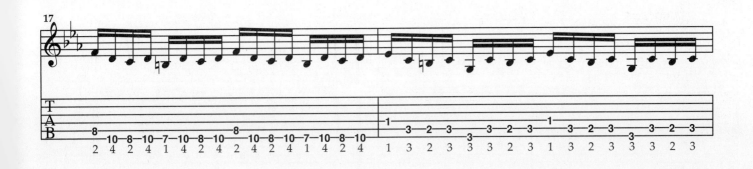

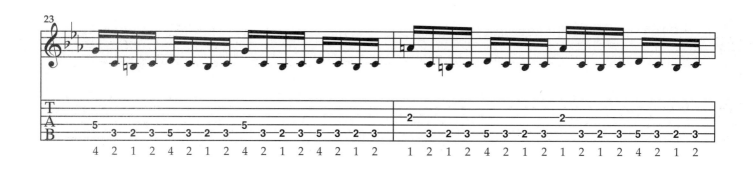

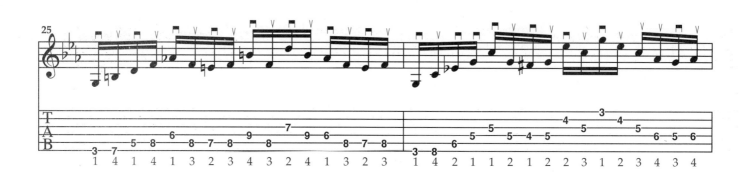

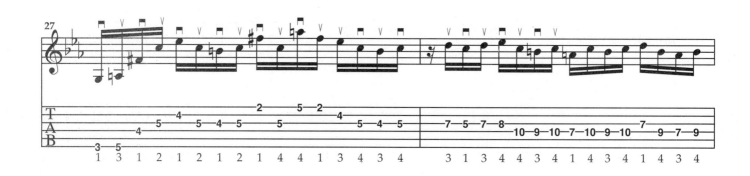

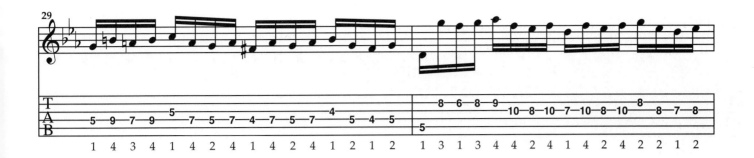

BADINERIE

Brief Musical Analysis

"Badinerie" (BWV 1067) was originally a piece for flute and orchestra from Bach's *Suite No. 2 in B Minor,* written around 1717. The meter of this piece is a lively $\frac{2}{4}$ (two beats per measure with the quarter note receiving the beat).

"Badinerie" is a great study for descending arpeggio runs, pedal points, and *staccato* (sharp, detached) playing. The main motif starts out with a descending arpeggio run in B Minor. This idea will be used throughout the piece on different chords, such as F♯ Minor, G Major, and A7.

Pay close attention to the sweep picking used in the following sequence. This will help you play this phrase fast and accurately. The arpeggio is divided into three different B Minor triads on the top three strings. The three triads actually comprise a larger, two-octave arpeggio. This fingering of the two-octave arpeggio will help you play the phrase cleanly and with rhythmic accuracy.

Measures 1–2

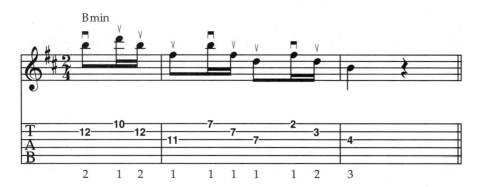

The second part of the motif (measures 2–4) is based on another arpeggio phrase that can be found in different variations throughout this piece. In the following example, a B Minor arpeggio leads to an F#7 arpeggio, which then leads back to the original B Minor phrase. This phrase has been arranged with a mixture of sweeping and alternate picking.

Measures 2–4

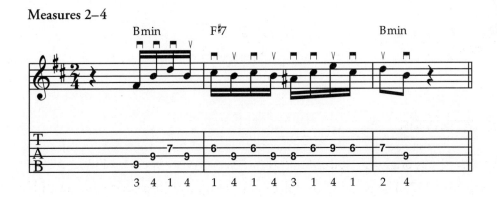

Measures 6 and 7 are very different from the melodic and technically challenging phrases throughout the rest of the piece, as it is a simple eighth-note line played staccato. The indication for staccato is a dot above or below the note. Staccato is a musical expression that tells you to play the note in a short, detached way. In some instances, the performer can apply slight palm muting to the strings, as it will help to bring out the clipped, sharp feel of the notes. Similar phrases can be found in measures 8–9 and 28–31.

Measures 6–7

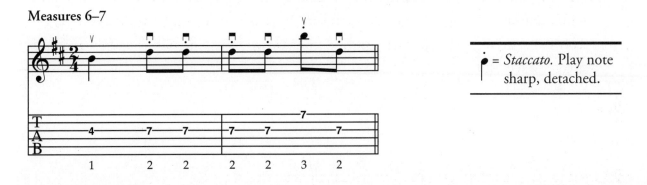

$\dot{\rho}$ = *Staccato.* Play note sharp, detached.

The next musical phrase, found in measures 12–16, is a great example of pedal point. Play it using strict alternate picking, and emphasize the ascending scale above the pedal figure (F#–E#–F#) with downstrokes on the high-E string.

Measures 12–16

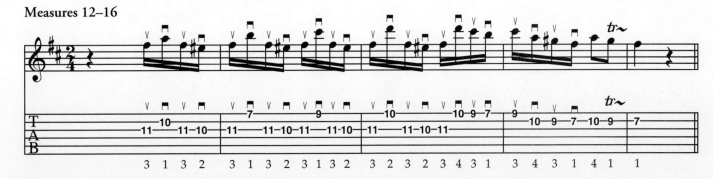

Measures 33 and 34 showcase fast, melodic, legato runs. Keep in mind that these runs lead into sustained melodic notes, and they should be played with rhythmic accuracy to ensure that the melody stays intact.

Measures 33–34

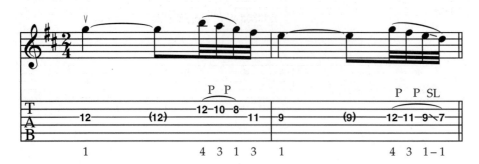

Measures 38–40 are to be played using a combination of sweeping and alternate picking. Harmonically simple, bars 39 to 40 conclude with an *authentic cadence* (a cadence ending with a dominant chord resolving to the tonic chord) from F#7 to B Minor.

Measures 38–40

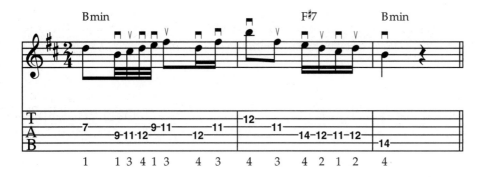

"Badinerie" is an elegant and wonderful piece that will enrich your Bach repertoire as well as your playing technique.

On Track 17, you will find the full arrangement. Tracks 18 and 19 are fast and slow backing tracks for you to practice over.

BADINERIE

(Continued on next page)

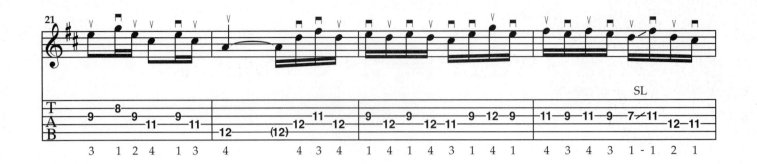

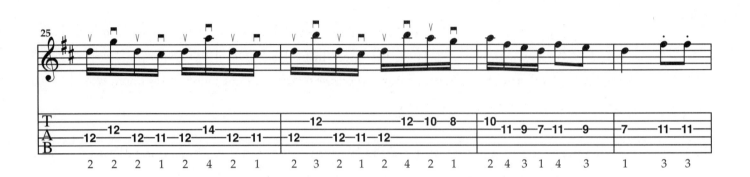

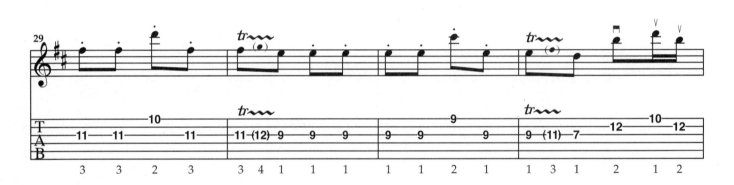

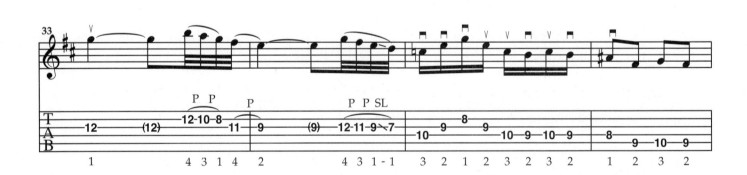

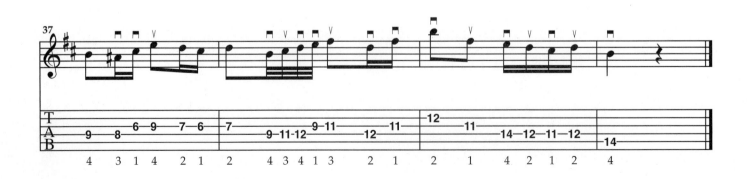

PRELUDE IN C MAJOR

Brief Musical Analysis

The "Prelude in C Major" (BWV 846) by J.S. Bach is undoubtedly one of the most famous keyboard pieces ever composed. It is the first piece in his book *The Well-Tempered Clavier,* written by Bach to prove his theory of *equal temperament.* There are 24 pieces in his book, two (major and minor) for every one of the 12 keys.

Equal temperament is a tuning system used in Western music, and it is based on the division of the octave into 12 equal half steps. Equal temperament made it possible to play in every key without sounding out of tune.

The basic motif of this prelude is a simple, ascending chord arpeggiation. In this book, the piece has been arranged using the tapping technique. You will not be using your pick at all.

Below is the main theme. Use a hammer-on-from-nowhere to sound the first note (C) then hammer-on to the second note (E). With the index finger of your right hand, tap the G on the same string. Now, with your fretting hand, hammer-on-from-nowhere to the C on the high-E string and hammer-on to the E note at the 12th fret. This phrase is then repeated for beats 3 and 4. Be sure to strive for a smooth and flowing feel.

Measure 1

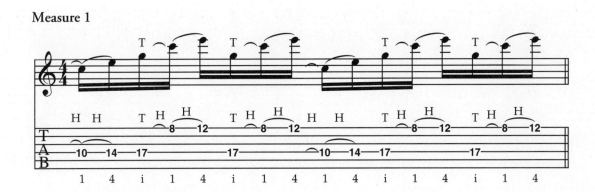

The next basic phrase (measure 10) is an arpeggio that utilizes larger intervals. However, this does not change the basic tapping idea. With your left hand, you will hammer-on-from-nowhere to the D and A notes on the 6th and 5th strings, then tap the D note on the 5th string. Following this, you will use left-hand hammer-ons-from-nowhere to sound the notes on the 3rd and 2nd strings, then tap the D note on the 5th string and use hammer-ons-from-nowhere to sound the F and C notes on the 3rd and 2nd strings. This two-beat phrase is then repeated.

Measure 10

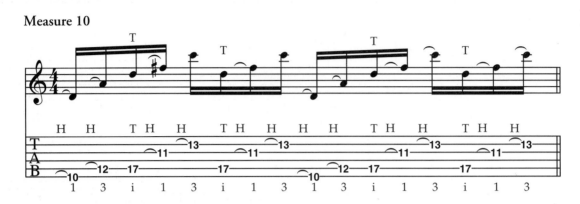

There is another variation to this pattern (measure 12). The next example shows that the fretting hand will hammer-on two notes on the A string before tapping.

Measure 12

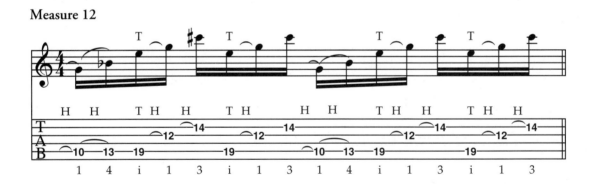

The chord progression of this piece features masterful *voice-leading*. Voice-leading involves transitioning between chords as smoothly as possible. These smooth transitions are accomplished by maintaining common notes between chords and moving the other notes upward or downward in the smallest intervals possible, usually a step or half step.

This prelude starts out in C Major and modulates to G Major, followed by F Major, and then closes in C Major, with a very lengthy *dominant pedal* preceding the final cadence. A dominant pedal is, typically, a short chord progression played over the root of the dominant chord that ends on the dominant chord itself.

Measures 33 and 34 are a simple F Major and G7 phrase played with tapping. Pay close attention to the fingering and tapping pattern, as it is slightly different from the rest of the piece.

Measures 33–34

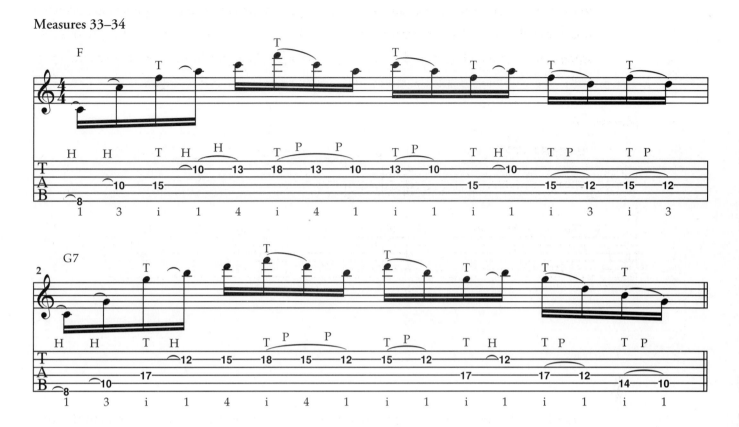

The final measure is a simple C Major arpeggio that is played in three octaves and ends on a high C.

Measure 35

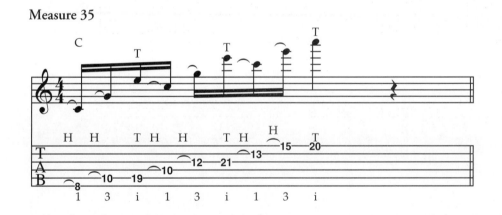

In order to perform this piece without unnecessary string noise or feedback when tapping, pull a soft hair-tie around the fretboard to dampen the strings. This is a common guitar-tapping accessory used by many players.

Try to practice this piece with only a slight overdrive sound on your amplifier. This will help bring out the clarity of the tapped notes better than with distortion.

On Track 20, you will find the entire arrangement. Tracks 21 and 22 are backing tracks for you to practice over.

Have fun!

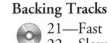
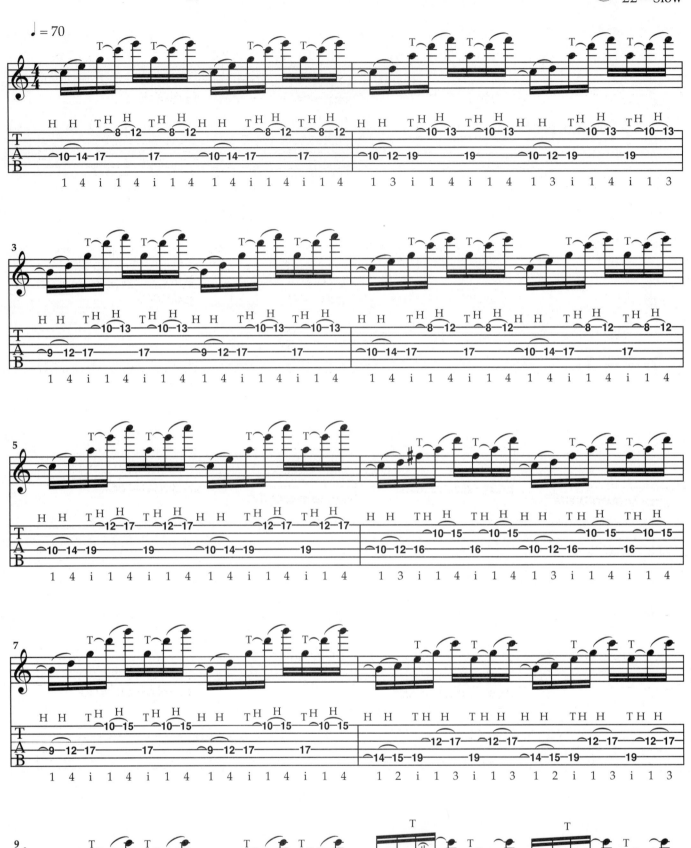

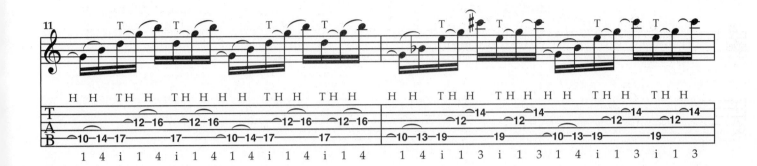

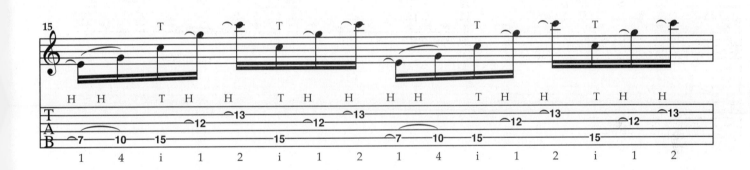

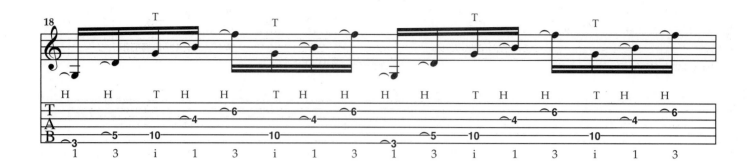

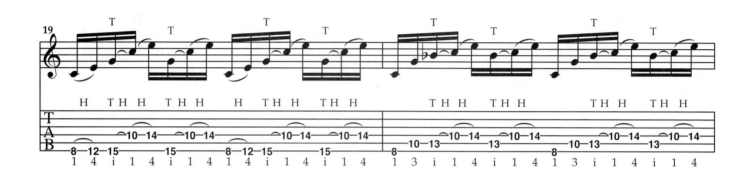

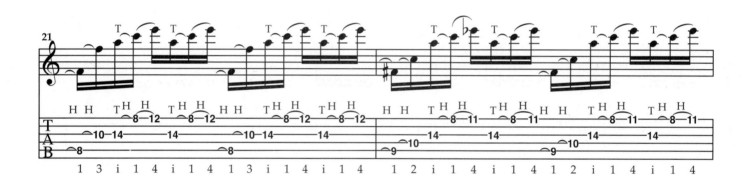

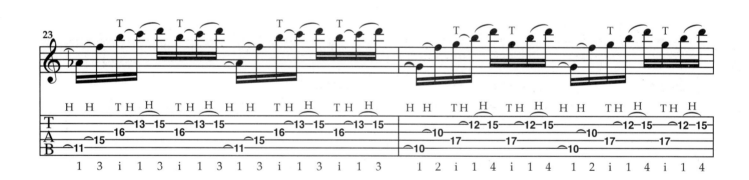

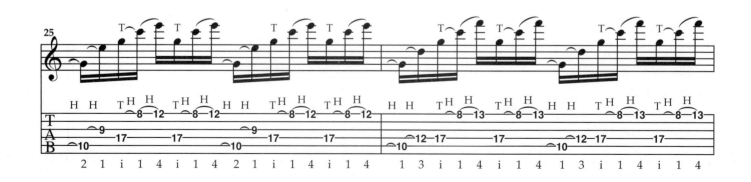

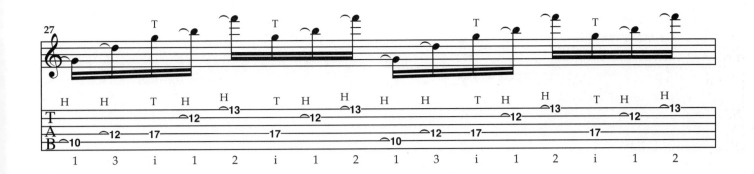

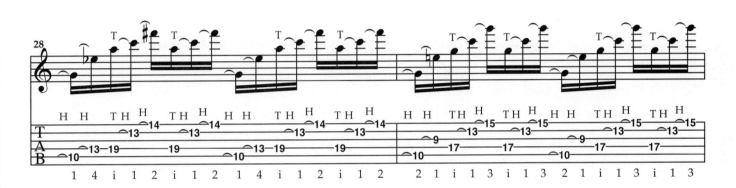

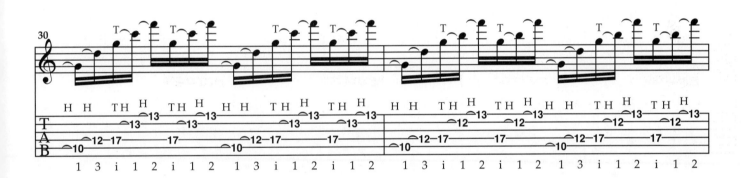

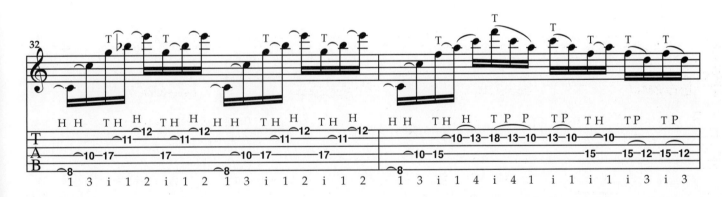

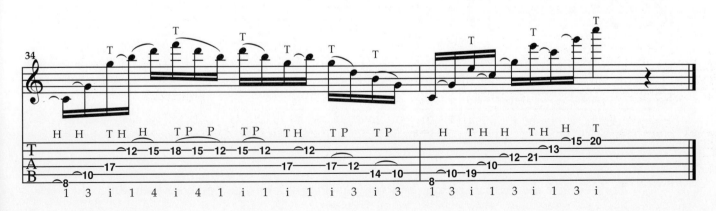

JESU, JOY OF MAN'S DESIRING

Brief Musical Analysis

"Jesu, Joy of Man's Desiring" is the 10th movement of the Bach cantata *Heart and Mouth and Deed and Life* (BWV 147). A cantata is a vocal composition with instrumental accompaniment. The piece is written in G Major and the meter is $\frac{9}{8}$ (nine beats per measure with the eighth note receiving the beat), giving it a smooth and very even feel, especially since most of this piece consists of a steady stream of eighth notes. In practice, the pulse in $\frac{9}{8}$ time is most often felt on the dotted quarter note (the duration of three eighth notes). With this feel, $\frac{9}{8}$ time can be thought of as having three pulses per measure.

The piece starts off with an eighth rest on beat 1 and continues with a constant stream of eighth notes. Pay close attention to measure 4, where the constant alternate picking is interrupted by a short sequence of sweep picking on beat 2.

Measures 1–4

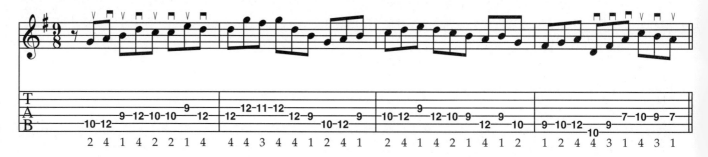

Measures 7 and 8 are another example of sweeping in this piece.

Measures 7–8

Try to isolate the alternate picking and sweep picking sections, and practice them diligently before connecting the different phrases. Make sure your picking technique is correct.

Starting from measure 17, the main theme is repeated one octave higher than in the preceding section. This transition is achieved smoothly through simple octave displacement of the repeated G note on beat 1.

Measure 17

This piece has been arranged to provide more variety and cover more of the fretboard. Measures 20 and 23–24 are exactly the same as measures 4 and 7–8 (discussed on the previous page), just one octave higher.

There are also slower melodic phrases in this piece, for example, in measures 9–11 and 14–15. When playing the longer, sustained notes, add some vibrato, as this will give your sound more ambience. This melody is repeated again in measures 25–27 and 30–31. This time, however, we'll include string bending.

Measures 25–26

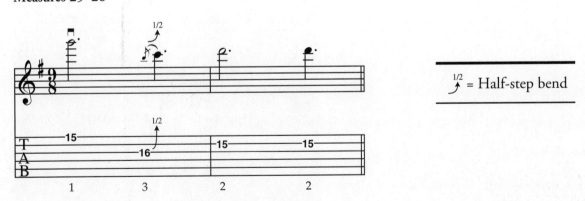

$\overset{1/2}{}$ = Half-step bend

The cantata ends with a fast, sweeping arpeggio sequence that ends on the high D. The last note is tapped by the index finger of your picking hand.

Measures 40–41

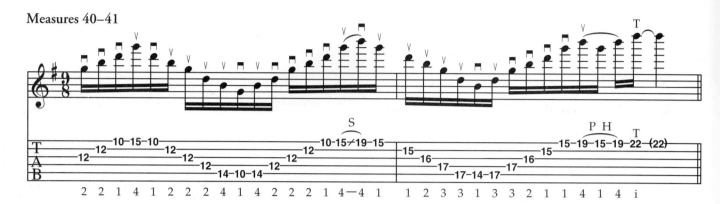

Practice this piece slowly and evenly, either with a metronome or the slow backing track for this piece (Track 25). This piece is a lot of fun to play and will certainly improve your picking technique and stamina.

Track 23 is the complete arrangement, and Tracks 24 and 25 are backing tracks for you to practice with.

Ritchie Blackmore (b. 1945) was a founding member of the groups Deep Purple and Rainbow. He was one of the first guitarists to innovate the "neo-classical" guitar style, which fuses blues and rock sensibilities with harmonic and melodic concepts borrowed from European classical music.

Jesu, Joy of Man's Desiring

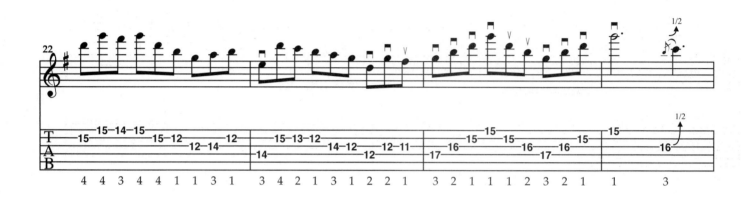

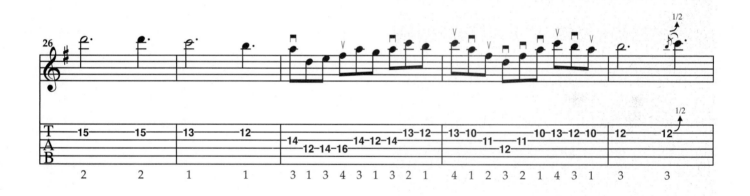

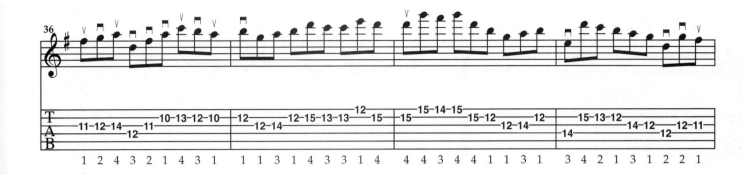

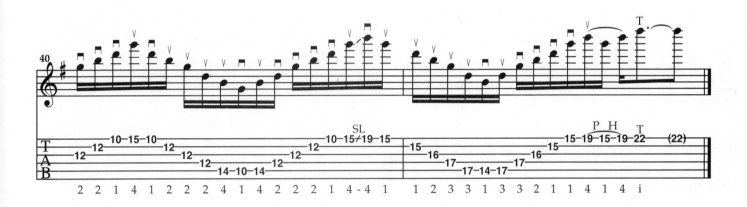

Starting with his debut album, Rising Force (released in 1984), Swedish guitarist **Yngwie Malmsteen** (b. 1963) took the neo-classical style to new heights with virtuosic heavy metal compositions, blazing-fast diminished and harmonic minor scale runs, and sweep-picked arpeggios.

AIR ON A G STRING

Brief Musical Analysis

The following piece by J. S. Bach is called "Air" (BWV 1068), but it is better known as "Air on a G String." The piece is from the *Orchestral Suite No. 3 in D Major,* and it stands out from the other pieces in this book because it is slower and uses other important melodic guitar techniques such as slides, vibrato, and smooth legato phrases.

The first statement of the theme is six-measures long. It opens with the following two-bar phrase, which contains a long, sustained note that resolves into an extended A Major arpeggio (starting on the "and" of beat 1 in the second measure).

Measures 1–2

The theme is restated (making this whole opening section 12 measures long) and then modulates to the key of the dominant A for the second part, starting in measure 13. This section features diminished arpeggios consisting of legato lines mixed with short, sweep-picking phrases.

The challenge with this section is maintaining the right timing for the sustained notes, as the piece is played at a slow pace. Performers tend to rush this piece and it loses its tension and dramatic resolutions.

Mcasures 13–14

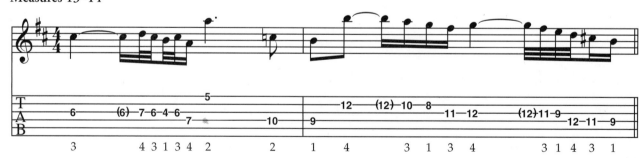

The majority of this composition is played using the legato technique. This smooth, fluid way of playing minimizes the sound of the pick attack. You can play the piece as written, but feel free to experiment with different combinations of hammer-ons, slides, and pull-offs.

The example below illustrates the use of sweep picking to accommodate the D7 and A7 arpeggios in measures 22 and 23. Pay close attention to the correct fingering, as it will help you to play this section smoothly.

Measures 22–23

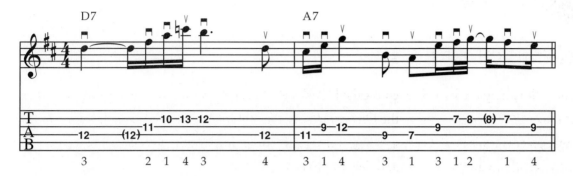

"Air on a G String" ends on a D Major chord in measure 24. Although this composition is vastly different from the other technically challenging music in this book, it presents a very different challenge that a lot of guitar players overlook: the development of touch, tone, and melodic timing. These qualities are very important to develop, as they will help bring your playing and creative skills to life.

Track 26 is the complete arrangement, and Tracks 27 and 28 are backing tracks for you to practice with.

AIR ON A G STRING

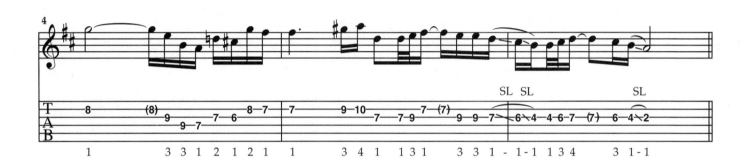

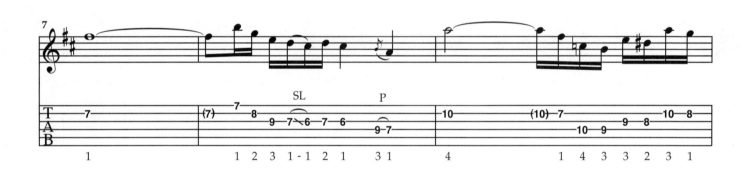

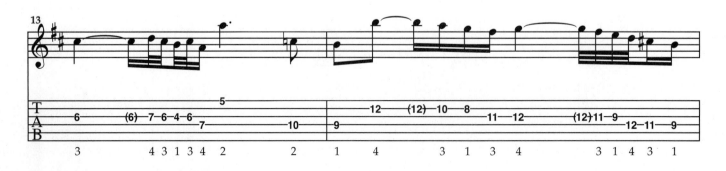

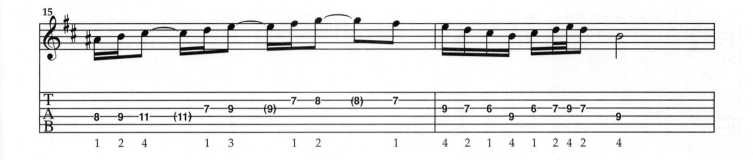

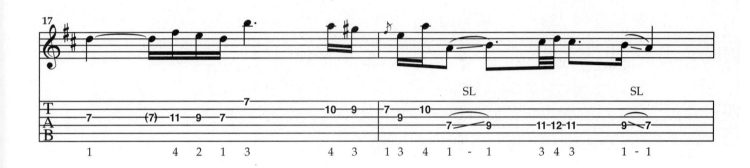

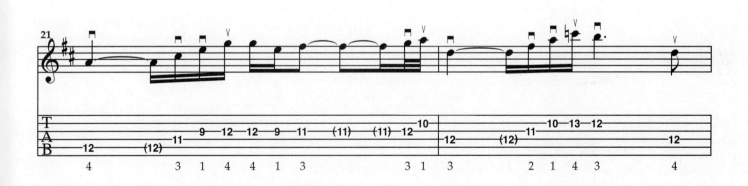

TOCCATA IN D MINOR

Brief Musical Analysis

One of the most famous organ works by J. S. Bach is the "Toccata and Fugue in D Minor" (BWV 565). This dramatic, epic piece has been featured in many movies, commercials, and video games.

The piece was composed sometime between 1703 and 1707. It consists of two sections: 1) the *toccata,* which is a free musical form that features the performer's virtuosity, and 2) the *fugue,* which is a strict musical form with many rules.

In this chapter, we will look at the toccata opening of this great organ piece. It begins with a short trill on the A note and is followed by a quick, descending scale run played with pull-offs. It continues with a variation of the basic theme, but one octave lower. The phrase starting in the second measure continues in a similar way and ends with a D Major chord in measure 3. (This is another example of the Picardy 3rd covered on page 31.)

There are several *fermatas* in the first seven measures of this piece. A fermata (⌒) is a symbol indicating that a note should be held longer than its normal duration.

⌒ = Fermata. Hold note longer than its normal duration.

Measures 1–2

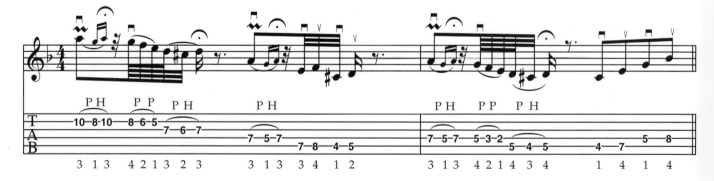

The next section is based on a rapid scale sequence that will be repeated again in measures 6 and 7, but one octave higher. Be especially careful when changing positions on beat 3 of measure 4, and beat 1 of measure 5.

Measures 3–5

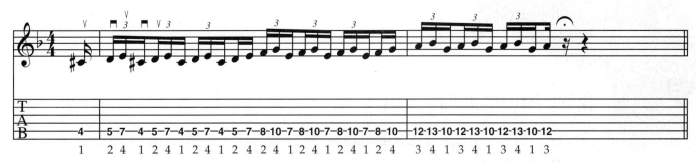

The next section (measures 8–10) features a cascading series of triads. It starts with E Diminished and is followed by D Minor, C♯ Diminished, B♭, A, G Minor, F, E Diminished, and C♯ Diminished.

This phrase utilizes the sweep picking technique, as it is the easiest way to play this rapid succession of notes.

Measure 8

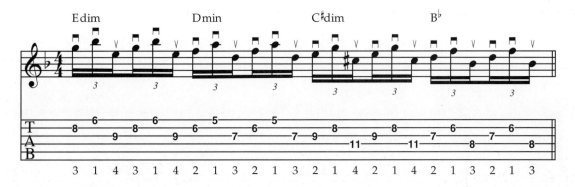

The next section (measures 12–13) consists of fast scale runs based on A7 and C♯ Diminished, and it ends with a D Minor phrase.

Measure 12 begins with a short D Minor arpeggio, which leads into a fast, ascending scale run on the high-E string. The phrase continues with a descending pattern of 3rds and 2nds.

Measures 12–13

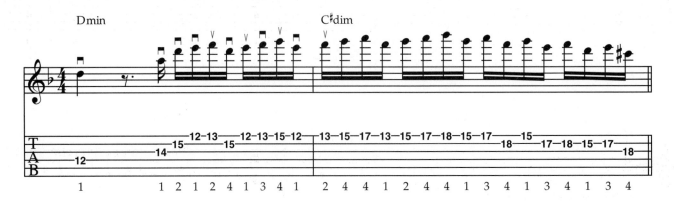

The descending pattern from above is then continued into two lower octaves (measures 14 and 15) until it ends on a Dsus4 chord resolving into a D Major chord with a trill on the 3rd. (A *sus4* chord is a chord that "suspends" the 3rd of the chord with the 4th, and it usually resolves to a major chord, although, sometimes, it will resolve to a minor chord.)

"Toccata" is a great solo piece for the guitar, showcasing many expressive technical features such as trills, fast alternate picking, sweeping, and much more.

Check out Track 29 for the musical example. This piece will not have a rhythm track or backing track because it is a solo piece that is performed in free time. Listen to each section and experiment.

TOCCATA IN D MINOR

Freely

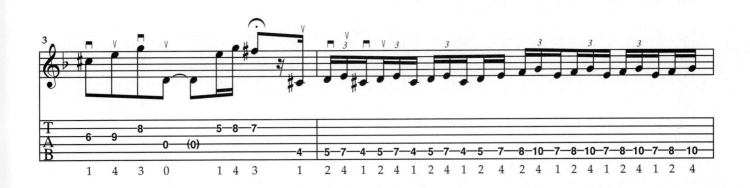

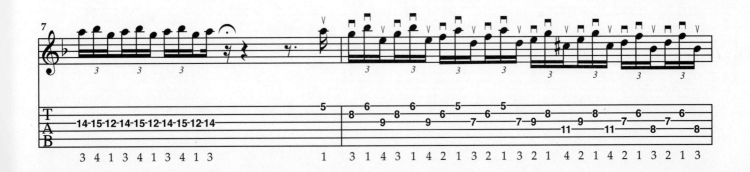

(Continued on next page)

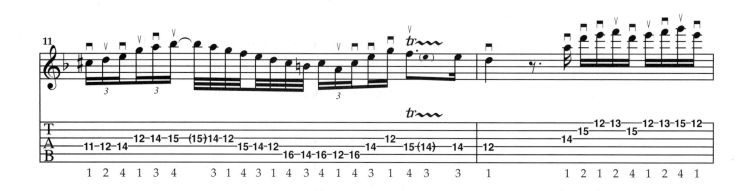

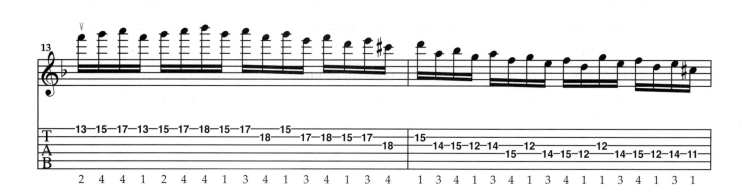

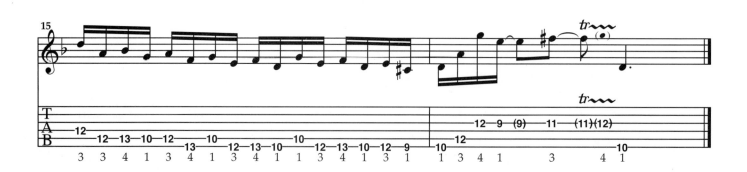

FINAL THOUGHTS

Bach's music is very challenging and complex, especially when it is arranged for an instrument other than what it was originally composed for, but it is well worth the effort!

Since this music is so challenging, it is advisable to warm up before attempting to play any of the pieces. As a general rule, it is important to warm up before practicing for an extended period of time; it is also important to take short, occasional breaks.

I would like to encourage you to commit to a regular practice regimen and schedule. Try to maintain a daily routine of technical and musical exercises, as this will help you achieve more technical facility and a deeper connection with your instrument.

Additionally, be creative, and try to take some of the licks and tricks from this book and use them to develop your own musical ideas. The wonderful thing about being a musician is that there is no end to what you can learn. There is always something new and exciting to discover. Mastering music is a lifelong process that takes study, practice, and discipline, but the amount of sweat you put into it is a small price to pay for the rich rewards it gives back to you.

Enjoy!